LEAD
WITH NO
APOLOGIES

21 WAYS TO BOOST YOUR INFLUENCE

JESSE A. COLE, JR.

Scripture quotations noted CEV are taken from the Contemporary English Version Copyright © 1991, 1992, 1995 by American Bible Society, Used by Permission.

Scripture quotations noted NKJV are taken from the New King James Version. Copyright © 1982 by Thomas Nelson, Inc. Used by permission. All rights reserved.

Scripture quotations noted MSG are taken from The Message. Copyright © by Eugene H. Peterson 1993, 1994, 1995, 1996, 2000, 2001, 2002. Used by permission of Tyndale House Publishers, Inc.

Scripture quotations noted (NIV) are taken from the New International Version®, NIV®. Copyright © 1973, 1978, 1984, 2011 by Biblica, Inc.™ Used by permission of Zondervan. All rights reserved worldwide. www.zondervan.com The "NIV" and "New International Version" are trademarks registered in the United States Patent and Trademark Office by Biblica, Inc.™

Kingdom Mogul Coaching
P.O. Box 442
Hazel Park, Michigan 48030
www.KingdomMogulCoaching.com

ISBN 13: 978-1-79-398913-0

Printed in the United States of America

DEDICATION

This book is dedicated to the leaders who struggle with owning their influence. Remember, you are more than enough. Your life is a template for others to build off of. There is someone waiting on you to
Lead With No Apologies!

"The first responsibility of a leader is to define reality. The last is to say thank you. In between, the leader is a servant."
-Max DePree

"Become the kind of leader that people would follow voluntarily; even if you had no title or position."
-Brian Tracy

"Before you are a leader, success is all about growing yourself. When you become a leader, success is all about growing others."
-Jack Welch

"Leadership is influence."
-John C. Maxwell

CONTENTS

INTRODUCTION

The path of an unapologetic leader is one that many refuse to take because it requires a sense of purpose, determination and focused energy. In most cases, they stand alone, waving the flag of leadership and declaring that life can be experienced at a greater level.

I've learned firsthand that unapologetic leadership is simply one's decision to own their experiences and use them to empower others. It is a practical, secure and efficient mindset. It's not perfect, but it's purposeful.

For a long time, I was insecure in my leadership abilities. When it was time to make hard decisions, I faded to the background. I remember feeling terrified when my high school basketball coach pulled me into his office and told me that my teammates were depending on me, and as team captain, I needed to be more confident in leading my them.

As a young man, I found myself being thrust into

leadership roles all of the time--from sports teams and choirs, to student leadership and faith-based ministry. I never sought leadership positions; the thought of leading scared me and I didn't want that type of attention. I was satisfied with just being part of the team. But, leadership always had a way of finding me. In some cases, you can't choose the people you want to lead; they choose you. Moments that need your special gift will find you, and how you respond to those moments will define you.

Finally, I embraced the call of leadership on my life. No longer could I hide or delay my true impact and cheat others, and myself, out of an opportunity to grow.

As I studied the art of leadership more and applied its principles to my life, I discovered that people are looking for someone with a sense of direction, consistency, the ability to offer innovative solutions to hard problems, and the ability to coach them to a better state in life. This type of leader isn't afraid to venture into the unknown for the sole purpose of returning with newfound values, which can increase the efficiency of others.

Unapologetic leaders aren't afraid to be active participants in what they believe. They understand that in order to create change, they have to engage with what needs to be improved.

They see the value in others and are secure enough in themselves to celebrate those around them. They have resolved to living life above mediocrity and because of their influence, others are inspired to do the same.

Lead With No Apologies is a collection of stories about people who found their leadership voice while in a crises and through triumph. Their stories prove that leadership development is a lifelong devotion. My hope is that as you study these pages, you will be able to answer the question, "What if I decided to lead with no apologies?"

"THE FIRST RESPONSIBILITY OF A LEADER IS TO DEFINE REALITY. THE LAST IS TO SAY THANK YOU. IN BETWEEN, THE LEADER IS A SERVANT."

-Max DePree

1

THE HEART OF AN UNAPOLOGETIC LEADER

It seemed like Stephanie's car broke down every other day. She knew that it was only a matter of time before she'd have to purchase a new vehicle, but it was taking her longer than she expected to save enough money for a down payment. Her car wasn't worth the hundreds of dollars it would take to repair it, so she decided to tough it out for a few more months, even if it meant that she had to ride until the wheels fell off.

On her way to work one morning, the car stalled on a main road. As the work traffic whizzed by, there she sat, frustrated and embarrassed, cursing the car, before realizing that it was not going to start back up and no one was coming to help her. So, reluctantly, she decided to push it to the nearest gas station, which was roughly a mile away.

She put the car in neutral, and with the driver's side door open, her feet on the ground and one hand on the steering wheel, she pushed the car up the road. Shortly after she started pushing, several other drivers parked their cars and joined her. Eventually, someone else stopped and offered to pull the car to the gas station with a chain that he had in his truck. This made the task a lot easier to endure, helping her to reach the gas station quicker and with less energy.

I heard a speaker once say that resources follow a mission that is already in motion. Leadership is not just something you can talk about; it has to be something that you do. It is functional. Operative. Practical. It requires movement.

A prerequisite of leadership is engagement. Dr. Myles Munroe, an international authority on leadership for the past 30 years, said, "In order to improve a situation, you have to engage it."

Many of the leadership titans of the Bible were already found doing the work when God called them.

Saul was so influential in destroying Christians that God decided to perform a total life hack, changing his name to Paul and using him to lead and build up His kingdom. He was instrumental in establishing churches, teaching God's people how to lead themselves.

Before being anointed as King of Israel, David was just a shepherd boy, leading sheep from mountainside to mountainside and protecting their lives from ravaging beast. He accomplished this with a slingshot and a heart full of courage.

Esther was just an ordinary adopted Jewish girl who honored the authority of her uncle. But after a nationwide beauty search and a royal makeover, she was chosen to be the queen of Persia, which gave her influence in a kingdom that stretched over 127 provinces.

When Jesus began to put together a team to

support Him in His mission of faith, love, grace and reconciliation, He chose men who weren't necessarily the most confident or spiritually skilled. But they were authentic and committed to their own individual trades of being expert fishermen. As He stood on the threshold of the sea and the sand, He announced that they would no longer be fishermen, but He would transform them into fishers of men.

God literally called all of these people as they were doing what they would normally do on a regular day. They weren't searching for the glory of men, but the glory of God found them.

The late San Diego Charger linebacker Junior Seau understood the significance of doing the work and being steady and committed. He said, "Leadership can't be fabricated...you can't fool the guys in the locker room. So when you talk about leadership, it comes with performance...and consistency."

Successful leadership is the result of active engagement and the focus on a singular mission. Some don't find it necessary to do the work, or they quit midway because the desire was never truly in their heart. Their motives were foul, or they didn't fully understand the magnitude of the mission. If the work isn't in your heart, then it won't be in your hands.

Next Steps: Think about the areas in your life that haven't been as fruitful as they could've been because your heart wasn't in it. Recommit your time and energy into making those places fertile again.

Declaration: Today, I will recommit my time and energy into establishing a regimen of productivity. I declare that I am gifted, and as long as I focus on doing the work of my passion, opportunities for advancement will find me.

Notes:

_____

_____

_____

_____

_____

_____

_____

_____

_____

_____

_____

"BECOME THE KIND OF LEADER THAT PEOPLE WOULD FOLLOW VOLUNTARILY; EVEN IF YOU HAD NO TITLE OF POSITION."

-BRIAN TRACY

2

DEFINE YOUR SUCCESS

In our culture, we are obsessed with winning. From middle school spelling bees to professional singing competitions, winning is the primary objective in everything that we do. Anything less than first place is considered unsuccessful. But how does one offer relief to those who rarely experience external victory?

What do you say to a child who has studied her vocabulary words for several months, only to receive a second-place award after her middle school spelling bee? How do you ease the agony of the middle-aged man who has been singing his entire life, only to lose the vocal competition to a teenager who isn't even half his senior?

Your particular problems may be more severe than receiving second place at a spelling bee or losing a singing competition, but if you are anything like these two people, you may feel as though you've been dealt a bad hand at some point. No matter what you do, you just can't seem to catch a break.

I totally understand. You're probably putting in hours of work and sacrificing daily to accomplish your goals. But when you compare your results to the success of those around you, you're not even close to matching their outcomes. Even King Solomon, one of the wisest men to ever walk the earth, suffered loss at times.

Solomon is believed to be the author of the book of Ecclesiastes. In Ecclesiastes 9:11, he said:

"Here is something else I have learned: The fastest runners and the greatest heroes don't always win races and battles. Wisdom, intelligence, and skill don't always make you healthy, rich, or popular. We each have our share

of bad luck." (CEV)

I don't think it is a coincidence that this passage is tagged in the book of Ecclesiastes, which can be interpreted as teacher. The chapter and verse is 9:11, which can be interpreted as an emergency. Could it be that God wants to communicate the sense of urgency concerning this matter?

I believe that He is trying to get us to understand that no matter who you are or what you do, misfortune is certain. Knowing this, you must determine what success looks like to you, or else you will never be fulfilled.

Life is interesting. One day you're having home-run experiences but then, when you least expect it, here comes a speeding curve ball that can force you out of position. But in the melee of your day-to-day endeavors, you have the opportunity to learn from life's curriculum. The good thing about being conscious of your experiences is that every time you increase your leadership capacity, you improve your self-hypothesis. When you can see your picture of success clearly, then you won't be intimidated by your failures nor manipulated by the apparent success of others. As a scholar of your experiences, you have a choice in how you share your leadership influence with the world. It is imperative that you own your success. Here are a few ways in which you can define victory for yourself.

Be vulnerable to God's direction

In our quest to be super-educated and respected by our peers, one can easily create a world of superficiality and false standards. Many times, we're striving to impress people who have no real interest in our soul. Following this path will eventually lead to emptiness and disappointment. When we define ourselves by the trends of society, we lend our trust to a system that doesn't have the ability to sustain us. However, when our picture of success is accompanied by God's presence, we can trust that He will magnify our results beyond our capability.

Jeremiah 29:11 speaks directly to our ability to trust God's plan versus our own. He is the architect of our purpose, and the success that was ordained for us is wrapped up in that purpose. Unfortunately, we don't know the full scope of His plan for us, but He has one.

Sometimes, it won't seem like it, but He truly has our best interest at heart. All of our steps are ordered by Him, even the missteps.

Seek to be effective

Work smarter, not harder. Your level of influence isn't defined by how many hours you work or how many people you manage. Albeit, I do subscribe to the 10,000-hour idea, I am more impressed with the leaders who make quality moves versus those who focus on the quantity of the moves they make. Jeff Haden says, "If you evaluate yourself by what you actually get done rather than the time it takes to get something done, you'll start to notice a difference in how you work."

Stay true to yourself

You've probably heard that success is not a destination; it's a journey. I agree. As you grow as a leader, your picture of success will evolve as well. You may find that what you thought to be success at an earlier stage of your life may no longer satisfy you in your current stage. That is why it is important to be conscious of what brings you fulfillment.

When I was a teenager, all I wanted to do was play basketball and create music. That is what made me happy, and that is what I was known for. Now, I am more concerned with encouraging leaders and providing for my family. I still love basketball and creating music, but I'm not fulfilled in those activities anymore. They are just things that I like to do. In this moment in my life, the only things that bring me fulfillment are creating content that increases the leadership capacity of leaders and making sure my family has the quality of life they deserve. Anything outside of those two priorities is secondary to me. I understand where I am right now, and I try my best to be there as much as possible. So, wherever you are right now, *be there*. Only give your time and energy to things that support that place.

Success is realized in moments, but it's appreciated over time. It is the result of continuous focus and action toward an expected end. Committing to this idea is a lifestyle.

Next Steps: Write down your beliefs about success.

Take a mental snapshot of what your beliefs look like. Start with this personal success statement: "Success to me is..." Recite your personal success statement out loud every morning for the next 21 days.

Declaration: I define my success. I will not allow others to impose their views of success upon me. When there is too much social noise, I will get quiet and refocus on what I know is important to me.

Notes:

_____

_____

_____

_____

_____

_____

_____

_____

_____

_____

"BEFORE YOU ARE A LEADER,
SUCCESS IS ALL ABOUT
GROWING YOURSELF. WHEN
BECOME A LEADER, SUCCESS IS
ALL ABOUT GROWING OTHERS."

-JACK WELCH

3

GOOD COMPANY

A few years ago, I had the opportunity to watch a robotics competition. One of the student leaders from my church was an aspiring engineer and the captain of his high school robotics team.

His school competed in the regional competition and he invited me to come. I promised him that I would but, unbeknownst to him, I only planned on staying for thirty minutes. I had never been to a robotics competition before, so I didn't know what to expect.

As I entered the gym, I saw a glass partition that reminded me of a hockey rink, and three-feet-tall robots in the middle of the rink, tossing inflatable shapes around an obstacle course. The purpose of this contest was to see which team could score the most points in the least amount of time.

Here is the part that intrigued me: each robot had its own strengths and weaknesses. At the end of the qualifying rounds, each team had an opportunity to partner with a rival team to help strengthen their weaknesses.

For instance, if my team's robot was fast but had an issue with accuracy, I would partner with a team whose robot ranked high in accuracy. This boosted the chances at scoring high in the competition for both teams.

Once I learned the concept, my 30-minute visit turned in to two hours. I even took a tour around the facility to get more familiar with how the robots were maintained.

After seeing the robots in action, I instantly became a fan; especially with the partnership aspect of the competition. It reminded me of marriage.

Let's face it. Men and women are as different as a rock and piece of bread. Men are taught to be tough and emotionless. Culturally, women are taught to have a softer touch. We couldn't be more different, yet we have been fashioned to complement one another. We balance each other out in more ways than one.

It's amazing that we were created with a different purpose and function but we fit together so well. There is a certain beauty in how this relationship has been engineered. This is the aspect I would like to build on for this chapter.

Forming good partnerships is like choosing the right companion to marry. Aside from the emotional aspects of a relationship, leaders look at what their potential partner can bring to the table. Take note of the qualities that your potential partner possesses that can enhance your life. Identify how you can enhance theirs. Ask yourself the following questions:

- **What do I need from this partner?**
- **Do they have the resources to support the vision?**
- **What are their expectations of me?**

- **Are they as committed as I am?**
- **Are there any external issues that can affect our partnership?**
- **Do I even need a partner?**

To experience the glory of the relationship, be mindful that you are in the rink because of your similarities; however, your strength as a team is magnified when you celebrate your differences. The partner that you choose is a reflection of the value you place on your leadership.

Next Steps: Be more deliberate in choosing your partners. Ask the tough questions. Just because the grass is green, doesn't mean that it's real.

Declaration: The level of my influence is contingent upon the types of partnerships I entertain. I believe that the right connections have the potential to elevate me to a place I may not be able to achieve on my own.

Notes:

_____

_____

_____

_____

_____

_____

_____

_____

_____

_____

_____

_____

"LEADERSHIP IS INFLUENCE."

-JOHN C. MAXWELL

4

BUILDING DOORS

Some time ago, I attended a leadership conference and the theme of the conference was "The Year of Opportunity". After looking at the word "opportunity" all weekend, I thought that there was more to the term than what met my eyes.

I was compelled to dig deeper to find a clearer meaning of this experience. What I found changed the course of my life and was the catalyst for my pursuit to be more influential. Here is what I found.

The first two letters of *OPPORTUNITY* are "O-P", which, according to multiple dictionary resources, is the abbreviation for "observatory post". Observatory post is defined as "a forward position, usually on high ground". It is often used in association with the military. The next four letters are "P-O-R-T", which can be defined as a place of connection or inspection. Think of an ocean bank or a place where ships dock. The last four letters of the word are "U-N-I-T-Y", which means "the state of being one".

So after combining these definitions, this is what was revealed to me: *Position yourself in such a way that you will be able to see, connect to and become one with a chance to fulfill your leadership destiny.*

Business philosopher, Milton Berle said, "If opportunity doesn't knock, build a door." Building doors means that you are able to take risks, make sober decisions, and stay focused during the turbulence of the process.

When you are knowledgeable of what your values, skills, strengths and areas of opportunity are, you can position yourself to accentuate them. Believe that the energy that you invest into becoming the leader you desire to be will pay off. You have the power to create a space for yourself, which will attract the very opportunities you need.

In the book, *The Art of War*, Sun Tzu talks about capitalizing on the moment. He says that, "...opportunities multiply as they are seized." I am confident that this principle can be applied to how you influence people. Having a healthy self-awareness of the landscape of your influence will result in you becoming a well-balanced leader.

Here are a few questions to consider as you boost your influence:

- **What am I passionate about?**

- **How can I use my passion to help people?**

- **What am I willing to labor and suffer for?**

- **What skills do I need to improve?**

- **What do people say I need to get better at doing?**

Once you've engaged in personal dialogue and meditated on the answers, you can formulate ideas to create opportunities around them. Opportunity may not always knock, but you have the tools and experience to create your own.

Next Steps: Answer the questions above truthfully. Make a list of your strengths and areas of opportunity. Once you have identified the strengths and areas of opportunity, search for opportunities to perfect them.

Declaration: I have the right mindset. I understand that success is not always immediate nor will it be handed to me. Therefore, I will continue to initiate my progress. I will not abandon the process and I will always look for ways to position myself for the best opportunities.

Notes:

_____

_____

_____

_____

_____

_____

_____

_____

_____

_____

"A LEADER TAKES PEOPLE WHERE THEY WANT TO GO. A GREAT LEADER TAKES PEOPLE WHERE THEY DON'T NECESSARILY WANT TO GO, BUT OUGHT TO BE."

-ROSALYN CARTER

5

MAXIMIZE YOUR OPPORTUNITIES

One of the greatest gifts a leader can receive is an opportunity. When you are presented with a chance to grow, it unlocks your consciousness to the freedom and clarity of your possibilities.

Opportunity is always present. Unfortunately, there are some who fail to recognize it for the lack of being prepared for it or, even worse, it wasn't presented to them like they'd envisioned. Thomas Edison was on to something when he informed us that, "Opportunity is missed by most people because it is dressed in overalls and looks like work."

To ensure that you are positioned to benefit from your opportunities, consider implementing the following controls: *Expand, Reduce and Customize.*

Expand

Expand your knowledge-base in the areas that you want to impact. Learn and implement new skills and disciplines that increase your value and extend your reach and influence. This may include attending conferences, taking classes, reading books, or investing in coaching. This can be critical to realizing all the value created by your leadership platform.

Reduce

Reduce the noise. In photography, too much noise in a picture can distort the beauty of the image. The same is true in your leadership. Condense the amount of unnecessary engagement so that you can focus on the things that move you closer to where you desire to be. Too many tasks can keep you from focusing on the critical things that support your growth as a leader. Activity, in and of itself, doesn't always constitute achievement. When you focus on the right type of activity, you can achieve the results that you desire.

Customize

Customizing involves modifying existing processes to ensure that you amplify your potential. This may include creating a survey for your organization to see what your people truly value, updating your contact list, or creating a niche product for a specific customer base.

Increasing your influence in these areas requires you to be open to the things that are relevant to who you want to be as a leader and the direction you want your influence to take you.

Here are a few more thoughts to consider as you expand your leadership knowledgebase. I refer to them as the 7 Laws of Managing Opportunity:

Law #1: The Law of Expectation

Opportunity is discovered by those who believe they deserve it.

Law #2: The Law of Subtraction

Opportunities are maximized when you subtract the elements that don't promote the desired result.

Law #3: The Law of Preparation

Opportunity comes to those who have cultivated and nurtured their territory.

Law #4: The Law of Priority

Opportunity responds best to a culture of order.

Law #5: The Law of Protection

Opportunity must be guarded for it to fully develop.

Law #6: The Law of Preservation

Opportunity grows exponentially when it is properly preserved.

Law # 7: The Law of Reaping & Return

Opportunity that is harvested must be shared.

If you are inexperienced in recognizing when to employ these controls, you may find yourself in the right place at the right time, but unable to take full advantage of the opportunities that exist in that environment. Managing your opportunities and knowing when to expand, reduce and customize is key as you develop into an unapologetic leader.

Next Steps: Write down how you can apply the Expand, Reduce and Customize controls to your life. Invest time into growing and strengthening the areas that you identify.

Declaration: I am growing in my knowledge of how to maximize opportunity. I am confident in my abilities, and I will continue to polish my skills so that I will be ready for the right opportunity when it arrives.

Notes:

_____

_____

_____

_____

_____

_____

_____

_____

_____

_____

_____

_____

_____

"LEADERSHIP IS AN ACTION, NOT
A POSITION."

-DONALD MCGANNON

6

COMMIT TO
THE NECESSARY

Commit is a robust term. It is not just something you do; it expresses who you are. It's an ideal that suggests you are dedicated to a particular cause no matter what the circumstance. Despite all distractions, you're going to see a project through to the end.

Husbands and wives exercise an outward display of their commitment to one another by reciting their vows on their wedding day. But once the tux has been returned and the makeup is scrubbed off, the authenticity of their pledge is tested in how they communicate their love and loyalty for one another on a daily basis. This communication is necessary in order for their marriage to be successful. Without it there's a chance that there will be unnecessary turbulence in the relationship.

Anytime there is an expectation of success, committing to the necessary is required. Pat Riley, legendary coach of the Ervin "Magic" Johnson lead Los Angeles Lakers and perhaps one of the NBA's greatest teachers, knew how important commitment was when he said, "There are only two options regarding commitment. You're either in or out. There's no such thing as life in between."

The necessary things are the responsibilities that position you to be able to profit and deliver. Often times leaders thwart their success because they haven't identified what's necessary to lead their teams. They believe that every task is urgent when in reality not every task is even necessary.

A simple way to identify the necessary assignments is to write down the end goal and work backwards. Why the end goal? Because that is the result you're striving for. You can't control time, and it's impossible to predict momentum, but you do have the authority to identify the necessary steps you need to take to accomplish a goal. Why exert massive amounts of energy when you haven't even acknowledged the desired result? The result is what matters. The result dictates the corresponding tasks.

After you've identified the end goal compose the various tasks needed to fulfill that goal. I typically write down everything I think needs to be done, I call this an *Idea Dump*. I list all the possible actions I think I need to take to accomplish the assignment. Afterwards, I begin to sift through the list to identify and dispose of the low yielding activity. Low yielding activity are the items that will cause me to look and *feel* productive but they don't deliver any real value to the goal. Focusing too much on them will only push you further away from your goal and delay your action toward the things that are critical to you achieving your desired reality. Anything that doesn't drive your result is just a distraction.

Once I've removed the low yielding activity I am then left with only the necessary tasks. These tasks influence my outcome in a major way. At this point it's all about prioritizing and assigning a deadline to the tasks and taking inventory of my resources to get the job done effectively.

If you attack this responsibility with fiery intention you will lessen your chances of future discomfort. These tasks usually require a great deal of your attention, but if not managed properly, they can have a damaging impact on your overall goal.

Committed leaders practice what is necessary to safeguard against disasters and increase their chances of success. I encourage you to stay committed to the necessary things.

Next Steps: Write down a goal that you would like to accomplish within the next 21 days. Under that goal, list all of the tasks you think you need to do to complete the goal. Then, eliminate any task that doesn't get you closer to your 21 day goal. Next, identify the necessary resources and set a deadline for each goal.

Declaration: Going forward, I will invest my time and energy into the things that drive my goals. I will not be preoccupied with menial tasks that bring little value to my objectives.

Notes:

_____

_____

_____

_____

_____

_____

_____

_____

_____

_____

"AVERAGE LEADERS RAISE THE BAR ON THEMSELVES; GOOD LEADERS RAISE THE BAR FOR OTHERS; GREAT LEADERS INSPIRE OTHERS TO RAISE THEIR OWN BAR."

-ORRIN WOODWARD

7

MENTORS MATTER

As a child, your sphere of influence was circumstantial. You were guided by whatever environment you were exposed to by your parents. Whether it was healthy or not, you didn't have much control over who impacted your life.

As an adult, your needs have evolved and you have the power to consciously choose who you allow to occupy your space.

Unfortunately, there are some who have yet to consider this truth. It's as if they have discounted their value, reducing their ability to attract quality relationships. Consequently, they cancel their chances at ever engaging in rewarding interactions--one's that are lucrative and inspiring, and those that stretch them to be a greater version of themselves.

I've heard that we are the average of the five people we spend the most time with. According to C.S. Lewis, the best way to gain wisdom is to associate with those who are wise.

Leaders are aware that their potential is contingent upon who they allow to influence them the most. That is why submitting oneself to a mentor are so important.

For a long time, I suffered because I didn't allow myself to be mentored by those who could help me develop into the leader that I knew I could be. I admired them from afar, but was too afraid to approach them because of my insecurities.

I convinced myself that these important individuals were too busy to invest in me, or that I didn't have enough experience to be mentored by them. I now realize that the seed of that mentality was the fear of rejection.

In reality, I knew I was worthy of their time and coaching. I had the social proof, bank statements from the investments in my personal development, and a library full of books to show that I was serious about developing into a greater leader. But the fear of not being valued kept me from reaching out to the people who could curtail my learning curve.

I failed to understand that the purpose of a mentor was not to judge me, but to offer me advice on how to get from where I was to where I wanted to be. Until I overcame those anxieties, I wasn't able to see the significance in choosing the right mentor.

Everyone doesn't have the aptitude to mentor you. Just because someone looks successful doesn't mean that they are the perfect fit.

The right mentors will help you discern what's coming, teach you how to prepare for it, and give you strategy on how to make it gainful for your life. They guide you and then take a step back so that you can learn how to walk on your own and take ownership of your success. More importantly, your mentor should align with your passion in some way.

Never be too proud to sit at someone else's feet for a season, even if it's virtually. Mentors are meant to help you P.A.S.S. in life. They remind you of your leadership *Purpose*, provide coaching to keep you on your *Assignment*, serve as a source of *Strength* when you need it, and keep you focused on your *Sweet Spot* so you remain effective in your efforts. You don't have to walk this path alone. There is a teacher waiting for you to show up so that they can deposit their leadership wisdom into your life.

Next Steps: Write down where you want to be as a leader in the next five years. Research individuals who have accomplished what you want to accomplish. Investigate their progress and get to know them from afar to see if they are the right fit. Send them a short email or hand-written letter to introduce yourself and why you admire them.

Declaration: Today, I detach myself from my feelings so that I can observe my circumstances from an elevated angle. I will be relentless in the reframing of my thinking to prepare myself to be mentored by the right person.

Notes:

_____

_____

_____

_____

_____

_____

_____

_____

_____

"WHEN EAGLES ARE SILENT,
PARROTS BEGIN TO CHATTER."

-WINSTON CHURCHILL

8

DON'T PLAY SMALL

Lynne has always enjoyed working with kids. After years of volunteering in the children's ministry at her church, she realized that teaching could possibly be an extension of her calling. After much encouragement from her husband, she enrolled in classes at a local college. Upon completing the certification program, she landed a job as a teacher's aide at a daycare center.

Lynne loved her work environment and cherished her fellow employees. But she always believed that she could do more for the children if she had her own facility. Providing for the children and performing at a high level was not an issue for her.

"I was getting paid on a regular basis, had health benefits and was consistently recognized as one of the top performers," she said. "But I knew, in the pit of my soul, that I could run a daycare facility because the work just came natural to me."

However, although she was proficient at her job, she lacked confidence to step out on her own and maximize her potential. She had never attempted to be her own boss. The more she thought about opening her own facility, the more fear and doubt seemed to come. She was constantly bombarded with anxiety-infested questions. How would she find other teachers to hire? How would she attract clientele? Was she competent enough to make sure the daycare was compliant with state regulations? Lynne couldn't see beyond the uncertainty, and she was sure that failure was imminent if she left the comfort of her day job. Her fear of failure became her confirmation.

Maybe you've been there before. You had a burning desire to accomplish a goal that seemed bigger than your ability, but you found yourself teetering on the ledge of destiny and demise. Or even more, like Lynne, you were stuck in a belief system that didn't foster big thinking. So, you became comfortable with settling for less. I've seen leaders with great potential accept the safest option, and they fail to move into a place where they can maximize their possibilities because they don't feel worthy. Author and business development consultant, Ann Marie Houghtailing, said, "People who don't feel worthy fail to advocate for themselves and instead take what is offered without asking for anything better."

To sheepishly accept the lesser option when you know there is a better option is unacceptable. It takes a bold person to command a higher expectation of themselves.

I'm happy to report that Lynne and her husband finally launched their daycare. They have created jobs for the community, a safe haven for children, and a source of stability for parents. They've even been showcased in their local media outlet for being ranked as one of the top daycares in their state. Although she was apprehensive in the beginning, Lynne knew that she deserved more than to be haunted by corrupted expectations. She didn't allow fear to influence her perception and weaken the power in what could be.

Deep down, you know that you were created to make an impact in your community, on your job, or even in the world at large. Your weaknesses don't cancel out your anointing to lead. Don't play small. Commission a life that is better than you could ever ask for or imagine.

Next Steps: In the notes section, write down the three areas in your life where you are playing small. Then write down a higher expectation (what you will do to step your game up) for those areas. For example:

Playing Small: *Not spending enough quality time with my spouse.* ***Higher Expectation:*** *I will dedicate 5 hours of quality time with my spouse this week.*

Declaration: I will live with a higher expectation. I have the confidence to use my experiences and resources to create the kind of life that I deserve to live.

Notes:

_____

_____

_____

_____

_____

_____

_____

_____

_____

_____

"A MAN WHO WANTS TO LEAD
THE ORCHESTRA MUST TURN HIS
BACK ON THE CROWD."
-MAX LUCADO

9

CHECK YOUR EGO

An unhealthy ego is the ultimate assassin to your influence. It is like a parasite, eating away at the innermost pockets of your soul and at the same time, infecting those you lead. Arguably, the seed of a corrupted ego is pride. One of the main components of pride is the need to be in control.

A prideful leader often employs vindictive schemes to control their environment. When their power is threatened, they risk losing authority. This, of course, is something a prideful leader wants to prevent at all cost. Because of their lack of genuine motives, they use their authority as a defense mechanism to shield off potential arrows that could possibly rip open their exterior and reveal their weaknesses.

For this same reason, they reject help, even when they need it the most. Eventually, their ego becomes a crutch to lean on if ever they sense failure approaching. This type of leader finds it difficult to be humble, therefore excusing their faults and mishaps as character flaws that others have to accommodate.

I've heard leaders say, "If they don't like how I do things, that is their problem, not mine!" Individuals like this usually look out for themselves at all cost. Seldom do they dedicate time to helping others reach their goals. Even if they do, their help typically isn't motivated by love and there are usually strings attached to the offer, which leads back to boosting their ego.

The apostle Paul reminds us in Philippians 2:3 that we should, *"Let nothing be done through selfish ambition or conceit...Let each of you look out not only for his own interests, but also for the interests of others."* (NKJV)

An unhealthy ego can cause a leader to decline new ideas that have the potential to trump his or her system. Any success outside of the leader's ideas leaves them feeling unaccomplished. Consequently, that insecurity shuts down the flow of innovation. When pride is active, it can drain the life out of promising possibilities.

Pride has a language all its own. It never considers the sensitivity of others and has the propensity to destroy trust and confidence. When it speaks, it says things like:

- **"I know everything I need to know. I don't need your help."**
- **"You must respect me no matter how I treat you."**
- **"I am better than you."**
- **"I'm never wrong."**
- **"You don't have the authority to hold me accountable for my actions."**

Thomas Merton said, "Pride makes us artificial and humility makes us real." Baruch Spinoza's evaluation is, "Pride is pleasure arising from a man's thinking too highly of himself." Lao Tzu acknowledges pride as a harmful, yet calculated status builder. "Pride attaches undue importance to the superiority of one's status in the eyes of others...When one sets his heart on being highly esteemed, and achieves such rating, then he is automatically involved in fear of losing his status."

Leaders often suffer for the people. Through that suffering, they gain more wisdom and become more equipped to lead. But an unchecked ego is not compatible with this conviction. It can simply destroy your chances at attracting the type of people who can add value to your life.

People want to be led by someone who is humble enough to understand their plight, yet skillful enough to help them find solutions. In order for leaders to do this effectively, they cannot be controlled by pride and ego. Leaders must always assess their motives and safeguard their influence from the vile trappings of these two iniquities.

Next Steps: Examine your thoughts and compare any prideful thinking to reality. Transform your irrational thoughts into realistic views by humbling yourself to this truth: You are responsible for developing leaders to be greater than you are.

Declaration: The depth of my influence is contingent upon how well I treat others.

Notes:

_____

_____

_____

_____

_____

_____

_____

_____

_____

_____

_____

_____

_____

"EARN YOUR LEADERSHIP EVERYDAY."

-MICHAEL JORDAN

10

SELFLESS BY DESIGN

Jose` is the chief volunteer coordinator for a non-profit organization that builds houses for underprivileged families. He has been a part of the company since its inception and enjoys his job immensely.

One day, after completing a service project, he heard a group of his volunteers discussing how they contributed to the work that day.

"I carried 50 two-by-fours today," one volunteer said. "Man, that's nothing. If it wasn't for me pouring the concrete, the driveway wouldn't have ever been completed," another man said.

This disgusted Jose` because the motives behind the conversation weren't congruent with the mission of the organization. Jose` was passionate about the work that he was a part of because it was bigger than the contribution of one or two people. After listening to the dialogue for a few more seconds, he decided to talk with the volunteers privately.

"Gentleman, first, I want to thank you for your help. Without you, this work could not get done. Secondly, I've been listening to your conversation and I'm disappointed with what I heard. I'd like to remind you that the one who humbles himself and serves is the one who does the greatest work. God is using us to build a house for a family in need. He could've chosen any group of people, but He chose us. I would like for you to remain in the spirit of service because what we're doing is the work of God."

Lately, I've noticed the increase in people who have adopted the idea that they are entitled to be served. From athletes and religious figures, to reality TV show stars and even coworkers, it seems like everyone wants to be served.

Marriages are suffering because of the spirit of servitude. Religious establishments are shifting, and even breaking up, because of this parasitic mentality. Leaders have been bamboozled into thinking that the more people that serve them, the greater they are. The purpose of what it means to have influence has been misrepresented.

Jose` was able to impact the volunteers because he had done the work himself. He modeled the type of behavior that made his service pure. The volunteers needed to keep this attitude in the forefront of their minds going forward because the depth of their influence depends solely on their ability to see the honor in serving others without boasting about it.

To quote social activist and boxing great, Muhammad Ali, "Service to others is the rent you pay for your room here on earth." Business philosopher Jim Rohn believed that "...whoever renders service to many puts himself in line for greatness..."

Great leaders often deny themselves privileges so that others might be served first. One must be genuine in their motives, giving of themselves with no expectation of return.

Service empowers the giver and inspires the receiver. It advances the mission of God through the medium of generosity. When leaders grasp this concept, their lives will be guided by the opportunities to improve upon the substance of humanity.

Next Steps: Research several service-oriented organizations in your community that align with your beliefs and life mission. Decide which one is the right fit for you and dedicate a few hours or more to helping further their mission.

Declaration: Regardless of my title or position, I am a servant first. I understand the value in serving others and I will use my time, talent and expertise to advance someone else's mission--and I will do so without boasting about it.

Notes:

_____

_____

_____

_____

_____

_____

_____

_____

_____

_____

_____

"THE SECRET TO LEADERSHIP IS SIMPLE: DO WHAT YOU BELIEVE IN. PAINT A PICTURE OF THE FUTURE. GO THERE. PEOPLE WILL FOLLOW."

-SETH GODIN

11

HANDS IN THE FIRE

Tiffany is the curator of the Venice Art Gallery, a small business that she launched 10 years ago where she sells her original paintings and sculptures. Before she was able to hire a staff, she handled every aspect of the business on her own. Like most entrepreneurs, she was the public relations director, chief marketer, manager of packaging and shipping, hostess, and administrative executive.

She now has two employees that share the responsibility of running the business and they enjoy the intimate work environment and being surrounded by her creations.

Tiffany finds pleasure in the day-to-day activity of refining her business. She is enthusiastic about training her team to be able to express the beauty of her pieces and provide her clients with the kind of service that keeps them loyal to her brand.

She believes that if her team is knowledgeable and confident, her clientele will be a reflection of that. This can result in seamless business transactions and more meaningful relationships with her clients. Because she was devoted to learning the various aspects of her business in her early years of building her gallery, she qualifies as the perfect adviser to her staff.

Whether you are the leader of a few or a few hundred, when you are willing to operate on multiple levels, you automatically raise the altitude of your influence.

An effective hands-on leader is not one who micro-manages or dictates. They create an environment where their people are skilled in their work and are so connected to the company's vision and mission that the leaders' presence is not a sign of distress, but of support.

Keeping your hands in the fire is all about being available. It requires you to model the behavior that you expect from your staff. This could include occasionally answering customer calls, sweeping the floor, or taking orders at the point of sale. Like a disc jockey, your hands are only in multiple places to make sure there is no break in the flow of the rhythm.

To be absorbed by the administrative aspect alone is detrimental to the culture and morale of those you've chosen to move your operation forward. One must make themselves accessible to their staff, coaching them and providing timely feedback. This shows that you value their time and are invested in their professional and personal development.

Mark Cuban, the owner of the Dallas Mavericks, said, "I'm not a micromanager, but I stay close to my employees to make sure I can trust them to do the work. Then I take a step back once they've proven they are competent."

Keeping your hands in the fire also means that you are a wealth resource. Staying abreast of the current hot topics, trends and progressions of your industry gives you the advantage. You must never allow yourself to drift too far away from your industry's border or the needs of your people. When a leader becomes detached from the soul of their people, they are in danger of losing their advantage and their people will begin to lose confidence in them.

Your influence and expertise help cultivate the collective values of your team and allows them to work in a secure and nurturing environment. Whether you have a less-driven staff person or highly productive individuals in your company, knowing how to position them for success requires a prescription of patience, tact and balance.

An effective leader pushes their people to accomplish their own level of success as they master their responsibilities, contributing greatly to the success of the organization.

Next Steps: Devote some time to celebrate your team this week. Share specifically why you appreciate them and how their individual efforts help further the collective vision and mission of the team.

Declaration: I will invest at least five hours this week into helping my team understand their value and how much I enjoy coaching them into expanding their leadership capacity.

Notes:

_____

_____

_____

_____

_____

_____

_____

_____

_____

_____

_____

_____

_____

"YOU HAVE TO BE BURNING WITH AN IDEA, OR A PROBLEM, OR A WRONG THAT YOU WANT TO RIGHT. IF YOU'RE NOT PASSIONATE ENOUGH FROM THE START, YOU'LL NEVER STICK IT OUT."

-STEVE JOBS

12

EMBRACE THE STING

Years ago, I had a conversation with my future self. Not a person who looked like me, but the real future version of me.

I was experiencing a period of great duress in which I was discouraged about the trajectory of my life. I was doing good work, and people seemed to be appreciative of my efforts, but I wasn't fulfilled. I didn't have the clarity that I longed for and I found myself reaching for opportunities that I thought would bring me gratification. However, they only clouded my vision even further. I was searching for an external solution, but instead, I found *me.*

Not just the physical me, but how I conducted business, treated my family, and presented myself to the world. The total expression of my core values and purpose was projected onto the screen of actuality. I was thrilled to see the complete version of the man I wanted to become.

That person did not allow mediocrity to taint his decisions. He operated in excellence and mastery. He didn't make excuses, nor did he settle for less than what he deserved. When I compared him to the person I was at that present time, I became disgusted with myself.

He illuminated the areas that I tried to throw shade on. That man exposed my inadequacies, not to embarrass me, but to call attention to the areas that needed improvement. What he revealed wasn't a surprise to me. I knew that I needed to improve. I recognized that I could do better, and that's why I had to embrace the sting.

The sting that I'm referring to is twofold. One feels it

when they are confronted with the challenge of growing beyond their sphere of familiarity. It is the feeling you get when you are faced with the reality that you have been playing small for so long that it has become your norm.

For some, the sting is translated into a sign of weakness and they become too afraid to overcome it. For others, the sting is a vehicle of motivation. It hurts, but it serves as the confirmation that it is time for them to step their game up.

Great leaders embrace the sting; they don't run away from it. They commit to the process of improvement because they understand that purification involves extrication.

Embracing the sting gradually disconnects you from mediocrity. At some point in time, every leader will engage in a dialogue with the better version of themselves. There is no escaping this exercise. Knowing that you need to improve in a specific area is one thing, but it's another thing to have your shortcomings pointed out by someone else--even if that someone else is your future self.

Next Steps: Be truthful about the areas you've been throwing shade on. Your team knows your faults, even if you never talk about them. Don't wait for people to be brave enough to tell you how you can improve as a leader. Take initiative and ask them, "What can I do now to become a more effective leader for you?"

Declaration: I will no longer willingly ignore my areas of opportunity. I will embrace the sting and learn from the process. I am a great person with awesome potential, and I am developing into the leader I was created to be.

Notes:

_____

_____

_____

_____

_____

_____

_____

_____

_____

_____

"GREAT LEADERS ARE ALMOST ALWAYS GREAT SIMPLIFIERS, WHO CAN CUT THROUGH ARGUMENT, DEBATE, AND DOUBT TO OFFER A SOLUTION EVERYBODY CAN UNDERSTAND."

-COLIN POWELL

13

THE ELEVATED PERSPECTIVE

A leader is often compared to an eagle. However, when discussing eagles and leaders, there always seems to be an exclusionary undertone associated with the connection, as if only a select few have the privilege of being great and possessing boundless vision.

Unfortunately, many have bought into that philosophy, therefore separating themselves from the very people they have been called to influence. Leaders scale the mountain of visionary control to investigate multiple opportunities to distribute to their team. They foresee the possibilities and communicate that information to those who can benefit from it the most. The way a leader frames his vision to his team is critical to the level of commitment they demonstrate.

It is important that the vision is communicated in such a way that it aligns with the core values of the individuals on the team. A leader's influence increases when he knows how to help his people see value in opportunities that speak to the center of who they are.

Doing this is not as easy as it sounds. It takes time and intricate consideration. However, there is a portion of unwarranted weight that accompanies this process. Not everyone will be receptive to you. As a matter of fact, according to the Pareto Principle, named after economist Vilfredo Pareto, only 20% of your team will do 80% of the work to make the vision a reality. While this may be an extreme example, it is very realistic.

In Ann Mars article, "13 Examples of the Pareto Principle", she states that in the domain of management, "There is usually a wide performance gap between the top achievers and the rest of your team."

Those who usually have the lowest performance outputs may try to make you responsible for their personal and professional growth. If your vision doesn't suit their agenda, they will deem you ineffective and will soon find someone else to lead them. What they fail to understand is that growth requires effort on their part as well.

Be careful not to allow this to discourage you. Your role in the equation is to see beyond the moment and provide the resources and leadership to move your team forward. Developing an elevated perspective takes time. You may have to endure some disappointments along the way, manage obstructions in workflow, discharge employees, and own a few failed projects. Persevering through these things will only make you more durable as a leader.

Leaders have the ability to see beyond the marginal setbacks and govern themselves accordingly. If that means you have to take a short sabbatical to regroup, feel free to do so. Sometimes you have to escape the chatter to get refreshed and remind yourself of what really matters. But don't stay away for too long. There are people depending on you to help them see larger possibilities.

Next Steps: Remind yourself why you do what you do. Ask your team if they are clear about your vision. Ask them to share how the vision and mission aligns with their core values. This will uncover what they find significance in and allows you to make adjustments, if needed.

Declaration: My vision is clear. My workflow is fluid. Unproductive energy, people or projects will not distract me. I have the ability to see beyond all marginal setbacks and distribute a wealth of value to my team.

Notes:

_____

_____

_____

_____

_____

_____

_____

_____

_____

_____

"IF I HAVE SEEN FARTHER THAN OTHERS, IT IS BECAUSE I WAS STANDING ON THE SHOULDER OF GIANTS."

-ISAAC NEWTON

14

MANAGING THE INFLUENCE OF OTHERS

Managing the influence of others is highly valued in relationships. When a person of great influence invests into your life or exposes you to a resource, they are in essence lending you their influence. Whether they are a friend, mentor or a manager, it is imperative that you handle their authority with care.

Brandon learned the value of handling the influence of others very well. As an up-and-coming motivational speaker, he had earned moderate local success from speaking at schools and small conferences, but had not been able to achieve his goal of presenting on national and international stages. After ten years of trying to make it on his own, he decided to invest in a speaker success coach, someone who knew the ropes and could give him insight into the business.

After six months of intense training, Mr. Dennison, Brandon's coach, reached out to the business manager of a gentleman who owned several multi-million dollar companies. One of his businesses was a VIP leadership firm that served as a mastermind group for CEOs. Every year, he hosted a two-day gala honoring the top 40 international businessmen and women. Mr. Dennison believed that Brandon could benefit from this experience, so he made arrangements for him to be one of the keynote speakers during the event.

Although this wasn't a paid engagement, Brandon was ecstatic about the opportunity. This event could possibly generate multiple national and international paid speaking engagements. Years of making cold calls, knocking on doors, and sending out press kits had finally paid off. All it took was one person to change the course of his career. He knew that working with Mr. Dennison would prepare him for the next level, and now he had a chance of a lifetime before him.

The day before his presentation, he snuck into the conference center so that he could meditate. With no one else in the room, he walked to the center of the stage, closed his eyes, took a deep breath, and pictured himself delivering his speech. He could already sense the excitement of the next day and wanted to do a great job, but he also hoped to make his coach proud. Because of Mr. Dennison, Brandon's life was not the same, and he wanted to make sure that he represented him well.

Managing the influence of others can do one of three things for you, if not all three. It pulls you into the present requirements of your destiny, it prepares you for your future, and it propels you further than you could ever go on your own.

Brandon was the beneficiary of each of these. Although he had put in the work, there was a new horizon of influence before him. Everything he did from this point on would impact his credibility and reflect on Mr. Dennison, too.

Long-term credibility cannot be bought. It must be earned. Never take it lightly when someone lends you their influence. Properly handling the influence of those who have a longer reach than you puts you in a position to build credibility with the lender and all of his resources.

Jamie Glass, President of Artful Thinkers and an expert in strategic sales and marketing says, "Influencers know they have the power to change or compel action...Those who sit closest to authority and are granted permission to persuade have a direct impact on your success."

Mr. Dennison was this person for Brandon, and now Brandon was responsible for making sure that Mr. Dennison didn't make a mistake by giving him access to an international stage.

Some leaders invest years into nurturing their sphere of influence. When they "let you in," this is their way of vouching for you. As they expose you to their sphere of influence, this drastically increases the value of your network.

Next Steps: Have you had a Mr. Dennison in your life? Did you manage their influence properly? If not, in the note's section, write down what you learned from that experience and how you've since grown. Also, write down how you will handle the opportunity if it ever comes around again. Afterward, go back and apologize to them for mishandling their influence if you haven't already done so. This may be the toughest part of completing the next step, but it may open up a new opportunity for you.

Declaration: I am a great steward of the influence of others.

Notes:

_____

_____

_____

_____

_____

_____

_____

_____

"LEADERSHIP IS NOT BULLYING AND LEADERSHIP IS NOT AGGRESSION. LEADERSHIP IS THE EXPECTATION THAT YOU CAN USE YOUR VOICE FOR GOOD, THAT YOU CAN MAKE THE WORLD A BETTER PLACE."

-SHERYL SANDBERG

15

PROTECT YOUR INFLUENCE

In my leadership development workshop, *Remove the Nouns*, I share a story about my father planting a vegetable garden in our backyard every year when I was young boy. I talk about how he would remove the debris from around the yard and then cultivate the ground to prepare it for the various seed.

After preparing the soil and embedding the seed, he built a makeshift fence out of chicken wire and drove wooden stakes into the ground to secure it in place. The fence was erected to deter the animals from feasting on the crops and ravaging the garden. He understood that the consequences of not protecting his investment would equate to a dreary yielding of his seed. Through this experience, I learned that anything of worth must be protected.

If your desire is to be an effective leader, *you* must set boundaries. A hard truth for most leaders is that even though we like to help people, sometimes we sacrifice too much of ourselves to do so.

University of Houston research professor and author of *I Thought It Was Just Me (but it isn't): Making the Journey from "What Will People Think?" to "I Am Enough",* Brene` Brown says, "Daring to set boundaries is about having the courage to love ourselves, even when we risk disappointing others."

Being too loose with your time and freely giving people unregulated access to your personal space is not an effective way to protect your influence. There is only one of you to go around. When you spread yourself too thin, you will not be able to offer the very best of you. Therefore, you shorten your reach.

A prerequisite to unapologetic leadership is to be clear on where you stand and what makes you uncomfortable. Being resilient in these two areas will help you counter anything that threatens your ability to be productive.

Allowing yourself to be overly accessible creates a lane for time abusers: people that incessantly take you away from accomplishing your objectives. You might find yourself solving problems that you've equipped them to solve on their own. However, because you've also trained them on how to handle your time, you have become their enabler. When you teach people that your time isn't valuable, it will be treated as such.

Anyone or anything that causes tension or unnecessary pressure is clearly not the best option to which you should dedicate your time. Don't allow that energy to dominate your space.

In her corporate training workshops, leadership trainer Dana Brownlee shares a story about a woman who was answering business emails while on her honeymoon. Dana's conclusion was, "If you don't respect your boundaries, nobody else will."

Here are several ways you can set boundaries that can keep you engaged with your people on a healthy level.

Take responsibility for the culture that you created

Leaders are the creators of culture. How your team functions, or dysfunctions, is because you've allowed it to happen. It may be time to tighten your bootstraps and introduce a corrective culture strategy, starting with you. Revisit the mission and vision of your team to determine what current behaviors or processes are in direct conflict with the beliefs of the organization. Once you've identified the toxic behavior, don't be afraid to initiate corrective action.

Identify your time abusers and slowly become less available to them

You don't have to send out a memo, post a status on social media, or even place a phone call. Just make the decision that your time is more valuable than what you've permitted, and don't allow anyone or anything to discount it.

Most people will get the picture and respect it.

Those who don't will protest. Regardless of the response you receive, *you* are the master of your calendar. Another form of time abuse is also unproductive habits that you willingly indulge in. The keyword here is *unproductive*. A few synonyms for unproductive are: *fruitless, sterile, barren, and idle.*

Similarly, these words are associated with death. Anything that you allow to abuse you will eventually kill your influence. What you feed the most will grow, and what you starve will eventually die. Starve all time abusers.

Be firm with your availability

Once you've decided to be more purposeful with your availability and mastering your calendar, watch out for the personal agenda activists who will try to wiggle their way in. Don't allow this to happen. Remind them of your mission and vision, and that your responsibility as a leader is to equip them to lead themselves. If they can't respect that, give them permission to be a part of someone else's team or organization.

Be secure in your decision. Realize that you can

only be your best when you're not stressed. Ultimately, you are there to lead others in word and deed. By setting boundaries and being firm in your availability, you teach your people to do the same for themselves.

Protecting your influence does not give you permission to be isolated from your team. Being untouchable is not the objective of this principle. Your team has to know that you are available to them. But by managing your availability, you help them understand the value of their training and your trust in their ability to conquer their daily matters.

Next Steps: Embrace personal responsibility for the culture that you've created, and design a plan of action to correct any dysfunction that is contrary to the beliefs of your organization. Identify the individuals and habits that can kill your influence. Become less available to them, and be confident in your decision to do so.

Declaration: To increase my influence, I must set boundaries. Being effective and available is important to me, but I will not allow anyone or anything to prevent me from being productive.

Notes:

_____

_____

_____

_____

_____

_____

_____

_____

_____

_____

_____

"YOU MUST BE THE CHANGE YOU WISH TO SEE IN THE WORLD."

-MAHATMA GANDHI

16

LEAD WITH NO APOLOGIES

Taylor works for a communications company in Nevada. She started out as a sales representative, but after only three years with the company her manager called her into his office for a meeting with the executive staff.

"Taylor," he said, "You've been productive beyond our expectation. You continue to exceed your quota and we feel like you've proven that you are a proficient sales woman. You have literally worked yourself out of your sales representative position. Because of that, we are offering you the director of sales position. We'll give you 24 hours to make your decision."

Taylor was stunned and excited about the offer and couldn't wait to tell her coworkers the good news. After the meeting, she walked back to her cubicle and hurriedly gathered her belongings before making her way down to the cafeteria where the rest of her team had gathered for lunch. She sat down at their table and listened to the conversation. It was the usual verbal protest against the establishment.

Noticing that Taylor was not engaged in the dialogue, Cathy, her cubicle mate, blurted out, "Taylor, are you ok? You're more quiet than usual."

"Yeah, I'm fine. I'm great. Actually," she gleamed, "I'm awesome. I just got offered a director of sales position!"

"Are you serious?" said Cathy. "I've been applying for that job for the last year and half. I've been working for this company for six years; you've only been here for three. That's scandalous!"

"I'm sorry you feel that way, Cathy. This is a great

opportunity and I'm really considering accepting the offer. I don't want this to cause a rift between us. Honestly, I couldn't wait to tell you because I thought you'd be excited for me."

"You thought wrong," Cathy said angrily. "I have more experience and seniority than you. This isn't fair."

I'm sure you can identify with this scenario on one level or another. You've paid your dues. An opportunity for advancement is placed in your hands, and you want to share the moment with the very people who have been in the trenches with you. You expect them to be happy for you but instead, their behavior indicates they are jealous and insulted.

Your first inclination may be to apologize for offending them. However, you cannot allow yourself to be dragged into the abyss of perpetual defense. Although at times you may have to admit to making bad choices, you never have to apologize for being a leader.

You will be tempted to grieve over those lost relationships. If you're not careful, you could find yourself downplaying your ability just to appease people and prove that you haven't changed with your success.

Once you've totally engaged with the fullness of your opportunity, you may see a separation from the people or environment around you. This usually doesn't happen because of anything you've done. It's just that, for reasons you can't explain, some people will change when your title changes. Don't feel obligated to keep those relationships. The people who are truly happy for you will continue to invest into your life without you prompting them to.

Some people find it hard to accept that they can be leaders because they've been trained to work toward someone else's measurements and ratings. There is no shame in committing yourself to someone else's vision. We all need someone to assist us along the way. However, you were created with a gift to lead in a certain area as well.

Leading with no apologies means that you have a deep conviction that drives you to accomplish your picture of success, even when it looks like you're the only one on the bus.

To lead unapologetically demands a power that persuades you to show up, even when no one else does. It is an inner peace that prompts you to entreat a higher influence when confronted with life's tough decisions. I can guarantee that you have been called to be an influencer, and there is nothing you can do to reverse it.

Many are called to lead, but few have accepted the call. When you've embraced the leader within, don't expect everyone to be excited for you. Stay consistent, even when people don't seem to like you. Once you have been convicted that you were called to lead, there is no room for shame.

Believe that you deserve it. Prepare your life to receive it. Center your energy into preserving it. Stay focused on the task at hand. Lead with compassion, conviction and common sense. Remain grounded in your values. Your duty is to go forth in power, continue to let your experiences educate you, and produce lasting results.

Next Steps: Refrain from apologizing for being called to lead. Continue to distribute excellence in everything you touch.

Declaration: I will continue to be persistent in my assignment. Although my position may change, the core of who I am will remain the same. I don't have to apologize for being called to lead.

Notes:

_____

_____

_____

_____

_____

_____

_____

_____

_____

_____

_____

_____

_____

_____

"DO THE DIFFICULT THINGS
WHILE THEY ARE EASY AND DO
THE GREAT THINGS WHILE THEY
ARE SMALL. A JOURNEY OF A
THOUSAND MILES MUST BEGIN
WITH A SINGLE STEP."

-LAO TZU

17

THROWING MOUNTAINS

Every leader encounters obstacles. That is the nature of what you do. You are a problem solver. A solution miner. The one who helps your people discover the answers within themselves. You can't hide from the hard stuff. Even if you try, it has a way of showing up in another domain.

The beauty is in how you fight through the challenges and eventually overcome them. You have no control over the momentum of overcoming, but you do have the authority to govern your words and actions as you overcome. The words themselves don't possess power. Having the gall to believe what you say and the willingness to move toward your desired result is what gives you the advantage to impact the lives of those you lead.

Possessing a firm belief that there is a solution, and then employing the proper disciplines to move toward that solution will set you on the path to attracting it.

In Matthew 21:20-22, Jesus demonstrated how powerful this principle is. When His disciples marveled at His ability to extract the life out of a fig tree with just words, Jesus replied, *"Truly I tell you, if you have faith and do not doubt, not only can you do what was done to the fig tree, but also you can say to this mountain, 'Go, throw yourself into the sea,' and it will be done. If you believe, you will receive whatever you ask for in prayer."* (NIV)

Leaders usually have big visions, but I can tell you from experience, sometimes believing only comes after speaking. On occasion, you will have to speak it *before* you believe it, until you believe it. Creating a synergy between your spirit, heart and mouth can be a challenge within itself. However, demonstrating this principle will eventually lead to you disabling any weapon of leadership destruction.

If you are a manager and you're having a hard time leading a disgruntled worker, don't depend on them to improve their behavior on their own. Speak what you need that employee to be for the company and provide them with the tools to become it. Not getting along with your spouse? Speak to them and treat them how you would if everything were as you desire. In both cases, over time, your influence can initiate change.

In the face of unconcealed hate, intercultural sabotage and political assassination, Dr. Martin Luther King, Jr. showed us how to throw mountains. During his marches, he led the song, "We Shall Overcome", but he had already overcome because he believed in a cause that was bigger than himself. He acted on what he believed in, even until death.

Throwing mountains involves a heavy dose of grit, determination and confidence that is selfless and purpose-driven. Unapologetic leaders respect the itinerary of that process. As you speak what you believe, the freedom and clarity of your possibilities will reveal themselves, even in the midst of the hurdles.

The hurdles aren't meant to deter you; they are but a reminder that you are still up and running. The race toward a better quality of life may be intense, but your knowledge, faith and ability to speak to life's challenges is broadening. You have the capacity to broadcast the content of your soul through your words. Be mindful of what you believe and say. As Jesus affirmed, saying what you believe and believing what you say gives you the ability to throw mountains.

Next Steps: While speaking to your obstacles, don't complain. Complaining designates you as the victim, and you will become so focused on the obstacle that you won't be able to see the solution. There is a purpose behind every experience. Ask yourself what lesson you can learn from your obstacles.

Declaration: As I learn to throw mountains, I will speak the solution that I want to see and find teachable moments in every challenge. My experiences are the solution to someone's problems.

Notes:

_____

_____

_____

_____

_____

_____

_____

_____

_____

_____

_____

"CHANGE WILL NOT COME IF WE WAIT FOR SOME OTHER PERSON, OR IF WE WAIT FOR SOME OTHER TIME. WE ARE THE ONES WE'VE BEEN WAITING FOR. WE ARE THE CHANGE THAT WE SEEK."

-BARACK OBAMA

18

CULTIVATE YOUR TERRITORY

A farmer will tell you that cultivating requires an insane amount of sweat equity. It is physically demanding and time consuming. But when done correctly, it provides a favorable nurturing environment for a seed.

In agriculture, cultivating involves breaking up the dry and rigid topsoil to uncover the fresh soil beneath the surface. It is also the act of nurturing, replenishing and developing the seed that was planted.

Life has a way of adding layers of desolation, causing you to be fallow and making it difficult to believe that you can be fruitful and influential. It will instigate thoughts that cause you to question your potency, discounting your ability to cultivate properly.

It takes a strong individual to exterminate that belief. Survey your surroundings to see what areas are bare, and address them like your life depends on it. You will get dirty, but you just might find some things that you never knew were there. As you dig, you may discover destructive habits that need to be reworked, unhealthy views that need to be healed, or some hurt from the past that was never confronted. Nevertheless, the confrontation is worth it for you to boost your influence. It prepares you for the process of leadership development.

Some people have tried to avoid the process altogether, yet they still expect to get the results of those who have toiled untiringly to be where they are. But like a plant with a weak root, they soon wither under the heat of leadership.

I like what the great cultivator George Washington Carver said about this: "There is no shortcut to achievement. Life requires thorough preparation -

veneer isn't worth anything."

You can't fake experience and preparation. Together, they give you substance. That substance, mixed with the favor of God, magnifies your impact and expands your territory. Your territory is your place of influence. It is the area that you have been given to nurture your leadership so that you can add value to the lives of others. Cultivating your territory is essential to increasing your leadership capacity.

One of my favorite affirmations is from Frederick Douglass. He said, "I prayed 20 years, but received no answer until I prayed with my legs." That is a powerful statement. It advises the leader to move from hoping to believing to becoming.

For the sake of those who glean from your influence, don't be afraid to get dirty. Cultivating your territory takes more than just wishing and praying that life were better; you are responsible for taking action.

Next Steps: Place yourself in environments that can alleviate your old unproductive views and awaken your passion to pursue greater things. Avail yourself to resources that can aid in self-evaluation and healing.

Declaration: I will devote my time and resources to cultivating my territory. I will not allow bad experiences to cause my terrain to become unusable. The pathway to boosting my influence requires that I internally identify my limitations and respond openly to the challenge of leadership development.

Notes:

_____

_____

_____

_____

_____

_____

_____

_____

_____

_____

_____

"MOUNTAINTOPS INSPIRE LEADERS BUT VALLEYS MATURE THEM."

-WINSTON CHURCHILL

19

ADAPT TO CHANGE

Robert works as a business coach for several startup companies. He has a steady travel schedule that keeps him busy enough to provide for his wife, Sabrina and their newborn son Ryan, but not so busy that he can't spend quality time with them.

After completing a successful week of sessions with a client, Robert headed to the airport to fly back home. After getting settled in at his departure gate, he called Sabrina to give her an update on his status. He was delighted to hear her voice, but her response to him was far from what he expected.

"Hello," she said. "Hi, sweetheart. I'm sitting at my gate. My flight leaves in about an hour and I should land around 7 p.m. I miss you and I can't wait to see you and the baby."

"We miss you too," she said. "It's been raining like crazy the past few hours. Our yard is flooded and, umm…our basement is flooded, too."

"What do you mean our basement is flooded?" Robert chimed in. "Everything in the basement is under water," explained Sabrina. "I'll text you a few pictures."

About a minute later, Robert received the text and he couldn't believe his eyes. Indeed, the entire basement was under water. His home office, furniture, personal items and appliances were all ruined.

After viewing the pictures, he took a few minutes to gather his thoughts. He didn't know the procedure of handling a flood, so he searched for articles online to figure out what to do next.

Once he gathered some information, he texted Sabrina back, "I'm sorry I'm not there with you right now. Don't panic. Stay away from the basement. I'm boarding my plane now. I will be home soon."

When he arrived, he kissed Sabrina and went directly to the basement stairs. Years of memories and hard work were now submerged under an ocean of city sewage. He sat on the steps and mapped out the next few days in his head. His priorities were to provide a sense of stability for Sabrina and their son, report the damage to the insurance company, and gather some man power to clean out the basement.

The next day, after Sabrina took more pictures of the damage, he and a few of his friends spent several hours hauling furniture and appliances and pumping water out of the basement. A few days later, the insurance company assessed the damage. Including the cost to replace everything and to restore the basement, the damages totaled over $30,000.

Certainly, Robert was confronted with a choice wherein he had to adapt to change quickly. Hence, you can learn a great deal from how he conducted himself in the midst of misfortune, and use that intelligence to increase your influence whenever you are in a vulnerable situation. When faced with tough leadership decisions, be mindful of the following:

Don't Panic

Don't get emotional. Emotions are like the water in Robert's basement--they shift with the circumstance. When tragedy strikes, confusion and frustration are usually left in its wake. Leaders generally make mistakes when they panic, but their influence grows when they maintain their composure during difficult times.

You can bet that Sabrina carefully observed Robert's reaction to their adversity, and Robert knew it, too. He was careful to gather himself before he texted her back to reassure her that their family would be fine. Being poised is a sign of your confidence in your abilities, and the assurance that a solution is present. Don't be moved by the madness.

Assess the Damage

Robert analyzed the situation thoroughly, viewing it from multiple perspectives. Subsequently, he was able to identify the uncertainties, expectations, limits and viewpoints of all parties involved. When you systematically investigate your tests, you will gain a multi-leveled panoramic interpretation, which can help you discover solutions that you couldn't identify on the surface.

Dive In

Although he had a dilemma, Robert understood that the burden was on his shoulders. He had to face the reality of his losses, clean up the damage, and move forward. Michael Myatt, leadership advisor to Fortune 500 CEO's explains, "...the only thing required to get beyond barriers is to stop complaining about the challenges and obstacles, and spend your time solving problems and creating outcome-based solutions."

When you are able to adapt, it exposes a fresh new world of opportunity to you. You just might uncover skills that you never knew you had. Baseball Hall of Famer Nolan Ryan offers his evaluation, "Enjoying success requires the ability to adapt. Only by being open to change will you have a true opportunity to get the most from your talent."

Every challenge presents a life lesson, and wisdom

often comes at the expense of discomfort. Adapting to change isn't easy, but sometimes getting through it involves getting dirty.

Next Steps: When an unexpected change arises, don't complain about the adversity. Assess the damage and search for solutions.

Declaration: In the midst of confusion and distraction, I will remain poised. My ability to adapt to change allows me to look past the boundaries and qualifies me to implement solutions.

Notes:

_____

_____

_____

_____

_____

_____

_____

_____

_____

_____

_____

_____

_____

"REAL LEADERSHIP IS LEADERS RECOGNIZING THAT THEY SERVE THE PEOPLE THAT THEY LEAD."

-PETE HOEKSTRA

20

IT'S A SET-UP

As a team leader, you make daily decisions about the working philosophy of your organization. Encouraging employee participation and empowering the people that you lead can result in your team members contributing their best effort. You can accomplish this by effective delegation.

One of the earliest documented examples of delegation is between a gentleman named Jethro and his son-in-law Moses.

Moses was charged with the task of leading an entire nation from a life rooted in four hundred years of oppression to one of total freedom, which could impact post-slavery generations. He was the mediator between God and His people.

While visiting Moses and seeing how he ran his operation, Jethro observed that there were no other leaders in place, besides Moses, who were handling the demands of the people.

This troubled Jethro to the point of him saying, *"...this is not a good thing."* He knew there was a chance that Moses' influence could deteriorate if he continued to lead in this manner. He believed there was a more efficient way of getting the work done and offered Moses a solution. Here is Jethro's recommendation according to Exodus 18:20-23:

"Your job is to teach them the rules and instructions, to show them how to live, what to do. And then you need to keep a sharp eye out for competent men—men who fear God, men of integrity, men who are incorruptible— and appoint them as leaders over groups organized by the thousand, by the hundred, by fifty, and by ten...They'll [only] bring the hard cases to you, but in the routine cases they'll be the judges. They

will share your load and that will make it easier for you. If you handle the work this way, you'll have the strength to carry out whatever God commands you, and the people...will flourish also." (MSG)

Jethro didn't doubt Moses' leadership ability; in fact, he was a priest and recognized God's influence in Moses' life. He was familiar with the burden that came with the job. Because Moses carried the weight alone, Jethro was concerned for his sanity and the people's ability to grow through his leadership.

In like manner, for a leader to thrive, his people have to be in positions where they can thrive as well. However, it is difficult to delegate when you see yourself as the sole carrier of the mission. It can be challenging to take your hands off of a project when you've been instrumental in creating the culture around it. Trust becomes a factor once other ideas and personalities are considered.

When making a decision to share liability, a few of a leader's concerns include: Will they do the job like I would? What are their motives? Will my influence be diminished? Will the work that I've put in be discounted? Is this person even qualified?

Jethro's example of delegating responsibility offers several leadership integrities that we can learn from. Consider the magnitude of your assignment and imagine how following Jethro's advice can impact your leadership, both qualitatively and quantitatively.

First, it is good for a leader to diagnose their inability to lead alone. The opening line from John Donne's famous poem, *No Man is an Island*, has been referenced on numerous occasions. However, the certainty that lies within the lines is worthy to be repeated, "No man is an island, entire of itself; every man is a piece of the continent."

In the grand scheme of things, we are all interconnected and everyone has a high competency in at least one domain. Thus, when a leader declines the opportunity to delegate a task to someone who could be of worthy assistance, he is rejecting the probability of working with a prospect who can bring a new level of genius to the team. In addition, he is setting the stage for potential frustration and will eventually bow to exhaustion.

But this doesn't have to be. A leader's DNA can be all over a project, but he doesn't have to use his own hands if he sets his people up properly. That doesn't give a leader permission to excuse himself from engaging in the work, but it does provide an opportunity to allow others to shine at his expense.

An unapologetic leader isn't too proud to let others shine. His motives are strategic and are rooted in the greater good of his team. How does one set up his people? Consider the S.T.A.M.P. model: Show, Teach, Affirm, Manage, Push.

Show

Show your partners exactly what you would like to see done, from the process to the results. Provide them with a written vision or picture of what the results look like. Team members tend to contribute more of themselves to a project when the assignment is clear.

Teach

Teach them how to do what you're asking them to do. Clearly explain the concept and reasoning behind the work, and provide them with the tools to excel.

Affirm

Affirm them in the process. This addresses the human need for feedback. Compliment them on the strides they are making toward the overall goal, but also advise them on their areas of opportunity.

Manage

Manage, when necessary. Healthy managing includes making yourself available to them for troubleshooting purposes. Because you have chosen competent individuals, be careful not to micromanage as it sends the message of mistrust, which can produce unnecessary tension amongst your team. When a leader is careful in whom he chooses, micromanaging becomes less of an issue.

Push

Push them to become greater. When people strive to achieve excellence, it creates an environment where support is at full capacity, innovation is without loss, and the mission is in full swing. But this cannot be realized when your team isn't being challenged. When your team becomes too comfortable, the mission and vision will suffer.

Although the goal is to complete a task, their leadership competency grows as well. Surely, distributing the load doesn't render you powerless; it gives you room to be even more influential.

Secondly, a leader must be wise in choosing who bears the load. Although the work may be too much for one person, it still requires delicate handling. Yes, the assignment is greater than its spokesperson, but only those who are qualified can align with it. Jethro's list was not a haphazard attempt at taking the pressure off of Moses for the time being, and it wasn't a freestyle solution.

His index of requirements was inspired by his catalogue of experience and authorized by God. Those who were potentially selected had to be competent enough to carry on the work once Moses' purpose was fulfilled.

Choosing competent leaders suggests that you have witnessed them investing time into learning the skills to lead, and they can discern the flow of the environment in which they work. When they fear God, have integrity, and are incorruptible, it implies that they are devoted to the intensity of their assignment and are less likely to compromise the integrity of the vision.

Lastly, knowing the heart of the candidate is an important aspect of delegation. It is easy to learn a skill, but a person can only hide their true self for so long. Leadership speaker, Simon T. Bailey, said, "...you hire for attitude, but you train for success." A person with the skill and moral stability that you need is nothing short of an asset. Invest in their professional development and watch them flourish.

Leaders cannot have a transactional approach when delegating tasks. There must be a value-added approach. A transaction only requires one to provide a service in a timely manner. It is not relationship-based and there is no concern about moral standards and beliefs.

In contrast, a value-added approach involves knowing the core of a person, what they find significance in, and how you can align those elements with the task at hand. Delegating is more than telling people what to do; it's giving the keys to the right people to do the work that they're already good at doing or have been trained to do.

Discern who can do what, and then position them to thrive in that area. Quick wins are good, but great leaders also set their people up for long-term success.

Next Steps: Diagnose your inability to lead alone. Recruit individuals who are coachable, competent, and have the character that aligns with the results you want to accomplish. Consider applying the S.T.A.M.P. Model to your leadership toolbox.

Declaration: The assignment that I have is bigger than what my individual ability can accomplish. I will surround myself with competent, incorruptible, God-fearing people who accentuate my strengths and are geniuses in their domain. I commit to developing and supporting them as well.

Notes:

_____

_____

_____

_____

_____

_____

_____

_____

_____

_____

"STRIVE NOT TO BE A SUCCESS,
BUT RATHER TO BE OF VALUE."

-ALBERT EINSTEIN

21

FINISH STRONG

The final marathon runner crossed the finish line. The last medal was awarded, and not too long afterward, supporters departed to their respective destinations. Just a few hours before, Olympic Stadium was packed with fans from all over the world that had come to Mexico City to experience the 1968 Summer Olympics.

It was approximately 7 pm. The remaining spectators and athletes were still buzzing around the stadium, basking in the ecstasy of the moment, when a voice resounded through the stadium speakers announcing the arrival of yet another runner. Confused about the broadcast, everyone fixed their eyes on the tunnel entrance. What happened next transformed the energy in the stadium.

As a figure emerged from the darkness of the tunnel onto the track, the ground lights revealed that it was John Stephen Akwhari, one of the marathon runners from Tanzania who had competed earlier, but did not finish because of an injury. During his scheduled race, he fell, hitting his head on the track, damaging his right knee. As he lay there in pain, the other runners trampled him. After he was carried off of the track, everyone assumed that his Olympic dreams were over, except John.

After a physical examination, and a few hours of recovery time, he convinced the doctors that he was okay to walk and he decided to go back to the track. In the presence of roughly one thousand fans, he hobbled along the track, dragging his leg in pain, determined to finish what he trained over four years to accomplish. After several painful minutes of limping around the track with a bloodied bandage wrapped around his right knee, he completed the race.

When asked why he came back to finish the race, he said, "My country did not send me over 11,000 kilometers to start a race. They sent me over 11,000 kilometers to finish one."

This was his defining moment, a chance to show the world that when a person is fixated on accomplishing a goal that is bigger than one's self, even at the expense of physical agony and social embarrassment, they set the stage to become legendary, cementing their legacy in time.

Your success as a leader is not determined by how you start, but how you finish. That doesn't give you the license to be careless in your preparation and planning, and I don't encourage investing in impulse-driven projects that can lead to unfinished tasks that clog up your time.

Whether you're in the beginning stages of starting a business, in a struggle to keep your marriage strong, or in the last semester of college, finishing strong builds your confidence for the next challenge and establishes a point of reference during those times when you feel like throwing in the towel.

Quitting is so easy to do. It takes very little effort to decide to give up. Equally, there is no pressure once you quit, and if you play your cards right, you can simply fade into obscurity and never have to live in the spotlight again. But just as you can decide to quit, you can also choose to conquer.

Effort requires a decision, whether the decision is to keep going or to give up. But God's intent for your life is not for you to fade into a realm of irrelevancy and insignificance; you were designed to shine. Strong finishers are contagious and inspiring. They radiate a light that draws others to the source of their strength.

Your strength is in God, and He isn't as concerned with the speed of your leadership development and influence as He is with your endurance. He is impressed with your stick-to-itiveness and your enthusiasm toward growth. His grace covers everything else that you can't sustain on our own. Here are a few ways to ensure that you finish strong.

Keep the vision before you

There is a story about an oppressed group of people

who dreamed of a new life and had the gall to journey thousands of miles across the ocean to find it. Once they settled in the new land, the first year they established a town. In the second year, they elected a town council. In their third year, their leaders proposed a plan to construct a five-mile long road that would stretch into the wilderness, giving them access to more territory to develop.

They were making sufficient progress, but in their fourth year, the citizens of the town tried to impeach the town council because they thought the road was a waste of their resources and would rather spend their time on other things.

How is it that just several years earlier, they had a vision to cross an unkind ocean to start a new life in an unfamiliar land, but now they were unable to venture a few miles into the wilderness to continue expanding their borders? When you lose sight of the overall vision, it can become easy to forget why you are running in the first place.

Stay focused

If you've ever watched the Kentucky Derby, you will see a piece of equipment on the horses head positioned on each side of its eyes called blinders. Blinders prevent the horse from being distracted by the other horses and help the horse stay focused on its own path. Allowing yourself to be preoccupied with the activities of others can be self-destructive. Focus on your core competencies and master what you do best.

Remain humble

Be honest about your limitations and be grateful for what you have, knowing that you couldn't have accomplished your goals on your own. Avoid being overtaken by vainglory; it's never too late to fall on your face.

Make prayer a priority

One may think that prayer requires hours of deep meditation. Certainly, that is a form of prayer. But, making prayer a priority is more about consistency and focus. Dedicate time throughout your day to offer thanksgiving to God. The fact that you are actually praying is an indication that you are blessed beyond measure. Prayer allows you to stay connected to the heavens while conquering in the earth.

Take time out to listen

Leaders are on the front line. So by the time challenges reach their people, it doesn't hurt as much as it could have. Though being on the front line isn't easy, and prayer can reduce the impact of the contact, remember to take time to listen. Sometimes, we can be so overwhelmed with our petitions that we forget to give God time to speak to us. He has mysteries to reveal, unsearchable truths. His strategy for your life can be heard in the silence of meditation.

The validity and impact of your legacy depends on your ability to finish strong. Using the celebrated words of Paul as an example can bring peace to your journey. He concludes in 2 Timothy 4:7, *"I have fought the good fight, I have finished the race, I have kept the faith."* (NIV)

Next Steps: Survey the areas in your leadership where you haven't been as disciplined as you could be. Pray for guidance in those areas and remain humble as you develop the skills to remain consistent.

Declaration: I am the righteousness of God. I am clothed in His favor. He has given me a vision for my life and I will remain focused in it. Communicating with God through prayer is my priority, and I will also devote time to listening to His instruction so that I can gain insight on how to finish strong.

Notes:

_____

_____

_____

_____

_____

_____

_____

_____

_____

_____

_____

CONCLUSION

Thank you for committing to your leadership development. Because you've invested in yourself, I believe that you have a genuine desire to lead unapologetically and increase your influence.

There is something to be said about a leader who is authentic. I've always believed that truth is not afraid of questions, nor does it have to defend itself. It just is.

The same applies to leaders who are genuine. We are constantly being watched, picked apart, and evaluated. Always remember that those who are influenced by you can sense when you aren't being sincere. Leaders must have a degree of transparency if they want to effectively engage with their team.

To them, your word is your bond. The absence of

genuine leadership leads to mistrust, and anything less is a mismanagement of your influence.

Will you make mistakes? Yes, you absolutely will; that's part of your growth. But true leaders possess the courage to admit when they have been inconsistent, and the capacity to correct their processes.

As you lead unapologetically, do it with a grace that causes your team to see Jesus and a tenacity that provokes the world to be inspired to do the same.

ABOUT THE AUTHOR

The CEO of Kingdom Mogul Coaching, LLC., Jesse encourages and equips leaders to become the better version of themselves. He believes that there is no separation between the work that you do and the reason you were created to do it. Embedding a faith component in every presentation, Cole teaches a framework that challenges company's to uncover the deeper purpose within their business and equips them with the tools to inspire their teams to perform at their optimum level. Cole believes that when a company is confident in what they offer, they can provide a more effective customer experience, which has a positive impact on their bottom line. Jesse is also the founder of the Michigan Institute for Student Leadership, a non-profit organization that teaches youth how to be more effective marketplace leaders.

MORE RESOURCES

AVAILABLE ON AMAZON.COM

COMING SOON

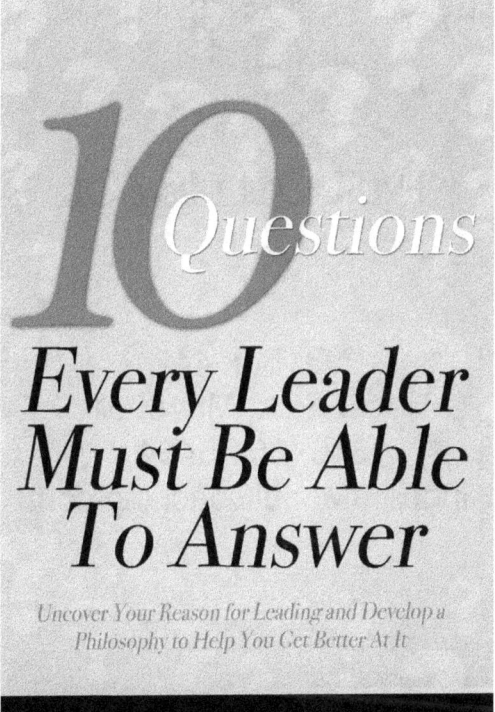

KINGDOM **MOGUL**
C O A C H I N G

P.O. Box 442
Hazel Park, MI 48091
(810) 354-5464
KingdomMogulCoaching.com

www.ingramcontent.com/pod-product-compliance
Lightning Source LLC
Chambersburg PA
CBHW071306220526
45468CB00001B/287

9 781793 989130